MW00513845

Natives and Newcomers

Georgia Southern University

Jack N. and Addie D. Averitt Lecture Series No. 3

Natives & Newcomers

ETHNIC SOUTHERNERS

AND SOUTHERN ETHNICS

George Brown Tindall

The University of Georgia Press

Athens and London

© 1995 by the University of Georgia Press
Athens, Georgia 30602
All rights reserved
Designed by Erin Kirk New
Set in 10/14 Baskerville by Tseng Information Systems, Inc.
Printed and bound by Thomson-Shore, Inc.

The paper in this book meets the guidelines for permanence
and durability of the Committee on Production Guidelines
for Book Longevity of the Council on Library Resources.

Printed in the United States of America
99 98 97 96 95   C   5 4 3 2 1

Library of Congress Cataloging in Publication Data

Tindall, George Brown.
    Natives and newcomers : ethnic Southerners and southern
ethnics / George Brown Tindall.
        p.   cm.
    "Georgia Southern University, Jack N. and Addie D. Averitt
lecture series no. 3."
    Includes bibliographical references and index.
    ISBN 0–8203–1655–5 (alk. paper)
    1. Ethnology—Southern States.   2. Southern States—
Population.   3. Southern States—Ethnic relations.
4. Southern States—Race relations.   I. Title.   II. Title: Jack N.
and Addie D. Averitt lecture series.
F220.A1T56   1995
305.8′00975—dc20   94-5970

British Library Cataloging in Publication Data available

Contents

Foreword

The faculty and students at Georgia Southern University were honored to have had Professor and Mrs. George B. Tindall as guests on campus October 5–6, 1992. Professor Tindall, whose books, articles, and lectures have had a profound influence on the historical scholarship of the late nineteenth and twentieth-century South, delivered the third annual Jack N. and Addie D. Averitt Lectures. His lectures, carefully crafted to appeal to students and academics alike, were both scholarly and entertaining.

Returning to the theme of ethnicity, the subject of his presidential address to the Southern Historical Association in 1973, Professor Tindall presented a commentary on the demographic, ethnic, and racial character of the South, a region long considered as home to a people of Anglo-Saxon descent and free from the tread of foreign races. Professor Tindall challenges this myth by demonstrating that in the colonial period the South's Indian, white, and black population was the most diverse in the English colonies. During the next two centuries the region became a true melting pot out of which emerged two new ethnic groups, one white and the other black. In recent years, the pattern has shifted back to diversity as Latinos, Asians, and a new wave of "Yankees" have moved into the South.

Professor Tindall's thesis seems especially timely for a contemporary South that must assimilate these newcomers into its well established biracial community. Because of these population shifts, a new generation of southern historians must address the issues of ethnicity and immigration and become involved in the debates over opposing theories of assimilation and pluralism. If Professor Tindall is right, the South is at a new juncture in its history.

A former graduate student aptly describes Professor Tindall's style as "alternatively playful and dead serious, always understated and wry, and always with an insightful turn that [takes] his work beyond the conventional." His lectures demonstrate anew his central understanding of the continuing tension between the forces of continuity and change in southern life and reiterate his memorable lines from *The Ethnic Southerners* (1976): We learn "time and time again from the southern past and the history of others that to change is not necessarily to disappear" or "to lose one's identity." To change "sometimes is to find it."

We express our gratitude to Dr. and Mrs. Averitt, whose generosity affords us the unique opportunity to bring renowned scholars such as Professor Tindall to campus. Others to whom special thanks are due include Professor Walter J. Fraser, Jr., chair, department of history, for counsel and encouragement, and professors Fred Brogdon, George Shriver, and Anastatia Sims, along with Esther Mallard, coordinator of special collections, who rendered faithful service as members of the lecture series committee. Peggy Smith, secretary extraordinaire, made my duties less burdensome by assisting with endless administrative details. We are indebted to Malcolm Call, director of the University of Georgia Press, for serving as an ex-officio adviser to the combined lecture committees and for guiding the manuscripts into print. Finally, we acknowledge those faculty members, students, invited guests, and townspeople who constituted attentive and responsive audiences for two days in October 1992.

R. F. Saunders, Jr., Chairman
Averitt Lecture Committee

Preface

On October 6–7, 1992, it was my privilege to deliver the Jack N. and Addie D. Averitt Lectures at Georgia Southern University. The essays that follow are revised versions of the original lectures, which were themselves drawn from a lecture delivered in Genoa on April 14, 1989, to a symposium organized by the Italian Committee for North American History. My subject there was the ethnic diversity of the South's people and especially the effects of the most recent immigration.

When delivered, the Averitt Lectures bore the title "The Multicultural South." At the time I used the word "multicultural" as a descriptive adjective in the meaning assigned by the *Oxford English Dictionary:* "Of, related to, or intended for several individual cultures"—or the slightly different definition given by the *American Heritage Dictionary:* "Of, relating to, or including several cultures." In common usage, however, "multiculturalism" has been deployed by so many different people in so many different ways that the word has become more puzzling than helpful. I hope that the title of the 1989 Genoa lecture, adopted here as an overall title for the Averitt lectures, states my purpose more clearly.

The lectures do not attempt to cover in detail the story of immigration into the South. They are chiefly commentaries, and they develop three main points.

First, in the colonial period the South developed the most polyglot population in the English colonies, encompassing Indian, white, and black peoples, with much diversity within each of these groups. The southern and western rims of the South, moreover, were occupied by Spanish and French colonists into the nineteenth century.

Second, in the two centuries after the American Revolution, relatively few immigrants came south, the Indian population was largely expelled, and the South became that part of the country where the melting pot worked best. Out of the crucibles of the South, two new ethnic groups emerged: white and black. These peoples might also be called a single group of ethnic southerners with white and black sub-groups that had more in common than they cared always to admit and that became more and more native-born as time passed.

Finally, after World War II a shift back toward greater diversity began when newcomers from abroad (now mostly Hispanics and Asians) and from the other states began entering the South in greater proportions than at any time since the colonial period.

Acknowledgments

Professors Valeria Gennaro Lerda of the University of Genoa and James L. Peacock III of the University of North Carolina at Chapel Hill first set me to thinking about ethnic groups in the South when they invited me to speak to conferences on the subject of ethnicity scheduled within a few days of each other in April 1989. The lectures printed herein are an enlargement on a single lecture, with the same title as this volume, that was delivered to each of the conferences in Chapel Hill and Genoa. That lecture was published in *From Melting Pot to Multiculturalism: The Evolution of Ethnic Relations in the United States and Canada,* edited by Valeria Gennaro Lerda (Rome: Bulzoni Editore, 1990), pp. 285–318.

For assistance in preparing that lecture and the ones included herein, I am indebted to the staff of the Reference Department of the Walter Davis Library at the University of North Carolina, Chapel Hill, especially to Bernice I. Bergup, Cynthia C. Adams, and Ridley Kessler, Jr., Federal Documents Librarian, and to the staff of the North Carolina Collection in the Louis Round Wilson Library,

Acknowledgments

also at the University of North Carolina, Chapel Hill, especially to H. G. Jones and to Alice R. Cotten. The index was prepared by Roberta A. Engleman of Chapel Hill, N.C.

During our stay in Statesboro, my wife Blossom and I were indebted especially to the program chairman, Professor R. F. Saunders, Jr., who served as our personal cicerone; to President Nicholas Henry for his hospitality; and to other members of the department of history, especially Walter J. Fraser, Jr., Esther R. Mallard, and Anastatia Sims; as well as to Professor Jack N. and Addie D. Averitt, who endowed this lecture series.

Natives and Newcomers

1
Natives and Newcomers

The South was a land of change long before the first Europeans and Africans arrived. Far from entering the virgin wilderness of legend, the newcomers entered a country in which the American Indians had for years burned forests and undergrowth to clear cropland and to make way for grasses, berries, and other forage for animals. The first-comers burned over their fields annually, a practice still widely followed in the southern countryside.

Such practices halted the normal forest progression toward hardwoods and created the stands of longleaf pine that still predominate in the Southern coastal plain. What is more, American Indian hunting practices produced the "greatest known loss of wild species" in American history.[1]

These lectures, delivered just one week before the quincentenary of Columbus's discovery of the New World, have a connection to that anniversary because they concern immigration to the New World, which began with Columbus. This is true if one ignores the fact that people had arrived thousands of years before Columbus. No one knows precisely when or how they came, but it is virtually certain from where. During the ice ages, they came from Siberia to Alaska, possibly across a land bridge left by receding water, across the ice, or perhaps by boat, and they spread southward.

One of the current survey textbooks in American history begins with a sentence I have long admired because it says more in six words than some writers say in six volumes: "The first American was an immigrant."[2] There is no evidence that *Homo sapiens* originated in the New World.

As we all know by now, some have assigned Columbus the burden of having brought sin to the New World. He was no paragon of virtue by current standards but by common report neither were the Carib Indians or Montezuma II. As a result of his discoveries, however, we now live in a world vastly altered from that into which Columbus was born.

In the 1920s and 1930s, my own native part of that New World—the South Carolina Upcountry—had become the staunchest repository of the Anglo-Saxon myth. In a book published in 1940 historian Ella Lonn set forth the outlook of the time by challenging it: "Probably no impression has been more deeply cherished by the population living south of Mason and Dixon's line and none more widely accepted by those who dwell north of that line than that which affirms that in the veins of the southerners flowed the purest Anglo-Saxon blood in the New World and that their soil was the freest from the tread of foreign races."[3]

It was as if one soaked up from the air one breathed the belief that the southern people comprised a population that was 99.44 percent pure Anglo-Saxon. Or was it pure Scotch-Irish? The two seemed oddly synonymous, a curious perception that appeared in print as late as 1972: "The Scotch-Irish early became Southerners. They were of the same Anglo-Saxon stock as the people of the coast regions."[4]

It dawned on me only much later that there was almost surely nowhere on earth such a thing as a pure Anglo-Saxon, or that Anglo-Saxon itself referred to an ethnic mixture that included elements other than Angles and Saxons—Jutes, for instance. Or that Scotch-Irish referred not to an ethnic mixture, but to Scots who had migrated first to Northern Ireland (Ulster) and then to North America and might more accurately have been called Ulster Scots but for the fact that they did not all come from there.

In the Greenville, South Carolina, of my childhood, the few examples of more recent immigration struck me simply as the rare exceptions that proved the rule: a Chinese laundryman who now and then came down to the family hardware store and took me next door for an ice-cream cone; a Greek restaurateur whose two sons were star pupils in the local schools and at Furman University; a "Syrian" (actually Lebanese) who ran a fruit stand up the street and whose daughter was a classmate in high school and college; and another "Syrian" who ran a grocery at the edge of a black neighborhood near my home. Much of the small population of Jewish merchants and professionals, at least the older generation, came from eastern Europe and spoke accented English. Each of these, you will notice, was a kind of ethnic stereotype incarnate.

Then there was the group that disproved the rule completely, if one thought to take notice. Blacks were a sizable minority in the Upcountry and far more visible than the few immigrants. More than that, they were a majority statewide in South Carolina until 1930 and in Mississippi until 1940.

But even in the coastal plain of South Carolina and Georgia, it was possible for most whites to be only dimly aware of black majorities and the rich Gullah dialect and culture of the Sea Islands and nearby mainland that owed much to an African heritage—among other things, this culture was the source of many words and place names that entered the English language. Many whites were also unaware that, although the first blacks arrived at Jamestown in 1619, South Carolina was the bottleneck through which about 40 percent of the African arrivals entered during the eighteenth century. Sullivan's Island, on the fringe of Charleston harbor and the site of a colonial quarantine center, was for blacks a colonial counterpart to the much later Ellis Island in New York Harbor and Angel Island in San Francisco Bay.[5]

The largest numbers of these newcomers were from the Congo-Angola and from Senegambia, but many were from the coast in between. The name *Gullah* derived most likely from Angola, although some believe it came from the Gola tribes of what is now Liberia on the Windward Coast.[6]

In the Upcountry I remained until high school ignorant of the fact that before the American Revolution my hillbilly home was part of the Cherokee lands. Nor did I suspect that in the colonial period my native state had such a polyglot mixture of natives and newcomers that as late as 1809 David Ramsay could write in his *History of South Carolina:* "So many and so various have been the sources from which Carolina has derived her population, that a considerable period must elapse, before the people amalgamate into a mass possessing an uniform national character."[7]

Already, however, Ramsay had detected, at least among whites, a melting pot at work, although of course he did not put it that way. "So much similarity prevails among the descendants of the early emigrants from the old world," he wrote, "that strangers cannot ascertain the original country of the ancestors of the present race."[8]

The process continued for nearly two centuries after Independence, and a considerable period elapsed during which southerners of diverse origins themselves evolved into a new ethnic group with white, black and American Indian subdivisions. So few newcomers were drawn south that a monumental study of southern demography in 1945 devoted less than 4 of 488 pages to immigrants, and those pages focused mainly on the origins of the South's population before 1850.[9]

In the *Fundamental Constitutions of Carolina* (1669) the Lords Proprietors tried to encourage immigration through a policy of religious toleration that gave Carolina a greater degree of indulgence (extending even to Jews and heathens) than either England or any other colony except Rhode Island and Pennsylvania. Very early this drew to Charleston a population of Sephardic Jews and French Protestants known as Huguenots, each of which made a mark on South Carolina more by their industry than by their numbers.[10]

In Georgia, the last of the colonies to be established, a band of 120 colonists founded Savannah in 1733. A group of refugees from Salzburg began arriving in 1734 followed by a number of German-speaking Moravians and Swiss, who made the colony for a time more German than English. The addition of Highland Scots, Portuguese Jews, Welsh, and others gave the early colony a multi-ethnic character greater than that of its neighbor across the river. Since the colony was a buffer against Spanish Florida, slaves and rum were excluded for reasons of security. These rules, however, were widely disregarded and finally abandoned in 1749. But Georgia never had a black majority.[11]

The colonial backcountry was settled in large part by a southward movement from Pennsylvania, where German immigrants lived in a buffer zone back of Philadelphia and the Scotch-Irish on farther out. Before the middle of the eighteenth century, however, the settlers came up against the barrier of the Appalachian Mountains and began to drift southward on the Great Philadelphia Wagon Road, which became the main route for migration to the backcountry, although some settlers came up from the coast. This road often followed old animal and Indian trails, as did the roads that branched off from it. For a large part of its distance the road simply enlarged the old Warriors' Path, used by the northern Iroquois and southern Cherokees alternately for purposes of warfare or for trade and communication.[12]

The Wagon Road led west from Philadelphia, crossed the Susquehanna River and led south through western Maryland, down the Shenandoah Valley of Virginia, and past Salem, North Carolina. At what was long known as the Trading Ford on the Yadkin River near Salisbury, the Wagon Road encountered an old Trading Path that had connected the Indians around the James River with the Cherokees and Catawbas to the southwest.

Just below the Yadkin the Trading Path became the main street of Salisbury and then led off in many directions with the main route coming down past Charlotte and then splitting into one route by way of Newberry, another by way of Camden, with both converging eventually at Augusta on the fall line. In the late twentieth century major highways and the main north-south railroad cross at the old Trading Ford and provide the routes along which the Piedmont Industrial Crescent has clustered. Off to one side a Duke Power plant has gone up.

At Big Lick (Roanoke), the Wilderness Road branched off into western Virginia, then on one fork down the

Holston River to Knoxville and on to Nashville and on the other fork west through the Cumberland Gap and back north into Kentucky. These routes, especially the Cumberland Gap, became major routes through the mountains and on to the Old Southwest. It was at Cumberland Gap that Frederick Jackson Turner, in his essay on the significance of the frontier, invited his readers to stand in imagination "and watch the procession of civilization single file—the buffalo following the trail to the salt springs, the Indian, the fur-trader and hunter, the cattle raiser, the pioneer farmer—and the frontier has passed by." [13]

Settlement in Rowan County, once all of northwestern North Carolina and later the vicinity of Salisbury, has been studied in great detail by Robert Ramsey in his book, *Carolina Cradle*. The mosaic pattern of Scotch-Irish and Germans, Ramsey finds, suggests the common pattern of the frontier with Scotch-Irish predominating over Germans and with both these groups joined by large numbers of English and smaller numbers of Welsh, French, and others. [14] There were, however, concentrations within certain areas. After their defeat in the Battle of Culloden in 1745, Highland Scots who had supported the Stuart pretender to the throne thronged to the Upper Cape Fear area centered in Fayetteville. There these largely Gaelic-speaking "45ers" encountered Lumbee Indians who had been speaking English for a century. The Gaelic tongue, however, along with German, lingered until the twentieth century. In the American Revolution these people remained mostly loyal to the crown, although they would have preferred to have a member of the Stuart family wearing it.[15]

Preponderantly German communities peopled by members of the Moravian Church appeared in the area around Salem, North Carolina, and German Lutherans settled in the area around the Dutch Fork between the Saluda and Broad Rivers in South Carolina, which included parts of Newberry and Lexington Counties. The Lutheran Newberry College still exists in the area. Both Salem and the Dutch Fork were located along the Wagon Road, but many of the migrants to the latter approached it from Charleston.[16]

There were unremembered Spanish and French settlers along the southern and western outskirts of what is now the United States. The Spanish established in Florida what is now the oldest city in the United States, St. Augustine (1565). In the coastal area north of St. Augustine during the years before the Jamestown settlement in 1607, the Spanish developed a series of missions and forts along the Georgia coast in a colony they called Guale, which stretched as far north as South Carolina. This effort eventually faded away, but the first settlers at Charleston in 1670 encountered Indians who spoke broken Spanish. About a century later the Spanish began establishing similar missions and garrisons up the coast of California, with more permanent results.[17]

Mobile (1702) and New Orleans (1718) were in sequence the capitals of French Louisiana, which claimed most of the Mississippi Valley. From 1763 until 1803, Louisiana was a Spanish colony that was then technically passed back to the French just before it was purchased by the United States. Both the French and Spanish languages eventually faded from the southern borderlands.

The outstanding exception was among the Louisiana Cajuns. The name was a corruption of "Acadian," after the French settlers expelled from Acadia in 1755 by its British captors, who renamed the territory Nova Scotia. Scattered among the English colonies, a large portion of the French settlers found their way to the remote bayous of south Louisiana where they preserved an archaic French akin to that of Molière and Louis XIV. By now most of them are long since bilingual, although most of them speak English with a distinctive accent.[18]

To focus on the white and black population, however, would be to lose sight of the fact that until about 1700, the first European colonists and their black slaves in the South confronted a majority population of Indians. The European invasion and conquest of America would have been far more difficult if the larger and stronger groups of the interior had occupied the Atlantic coast, groups like the Iroquois Confederation in the North and the Cherokees and Creeks in the South instead of the weaker Powhatan Confederacy, the Tuscaroras, the Yamassees, and many others. But Indians remained an important presence until the 1830s when Andrew Jackson's Indian Removal policy expelled all but a remnant from the Southeast, with most of them relocating in Oklahoma.

In the Ohio Valley–Great Lakes region, the flow of white settlement pushed most Indians westward before it. In the Old Southwest, by contrast, settlement moved across Kentucky and Tennessee and down the Mississippi, surrounding the Cherokees, Creeks, Choctaws, and Chickasaws and leaving the Seminoles (an offshoot of the Creeks) isolated in Florida.

These tribes in some part took on features of the white society. The Cherokees even had such trappings of white civilization as a constitution, a written language, and black slaves. Andrew Jackson, nevertheless, was fully in accord with the view that a "just, humane, liberal policy toward Indians" dictated their removal to the plains west of the Mississippi where they could remain undisturbed on lands then thought to be a desert nobody else would want. By 1835 President Jackson was able to announce that the southern tribes were gone or were in the process of being transferred mainly into the Indian Territory that later became Oklahoma.

Some groups and individuals, however, evaded removal, especially a group of Cherokees who later acquired land in North Carolina. In Florida the Seminoles fought a protracted guerrilla war in the Everglades from 1835 to 1842, but most of the vigor went out of their resistance when their leader, Osceola, was seized by treachery under a flag of truce to die a prisoner at Fort Moultrie, near Charleston. A few hundred Seminoles hid out in the swamps, and a scattered few of Creeks, Choctaws, Chickasaws, and smaller groups remained in the Southeast.[19]

During the eighteenth century the South, with its mixture of Indian tribes, whites, and blacks, had the most polyglot population in the English colonies. But sixty years after the Revolution the region had expelled most of the Indians, and the growth of the white and black populations came about mainly through natural increase. The Revolutionary War, followed a decade later by the French Revolution and Napoleonic Wars, interrupted immigration until after 1815.

In 1815, shortly after Congress outlawed the slave trade, the end of the Napoleonic Wars reopened the way for immigration from Europe. Thereafter, immigration picked up until, in proportion to population, it reached its antebellum peak in the years 1845 to 1854 when the greatest proportionate influx of immigrants in American history occurred with the arrival of nearly 3 million people, or about 17.2 percent of the total population in 1840. An even larger number of immigrants arrived immediately after the Civil War, and immigration reached a peak during the three decades after 1880.[20] The 1860 census showed that one of eight people in the country was foreign born. Most of the immigrants were Irish, followed closely in number by Germans and British. There were smaller numbers of Scandinavians and, in the far West, a few Chinese who, like the Irish in the East, were doing the heavy work of construction. After the Civil War the source of immigrants became increasingly eastern and southern Europe, which brought in rapidly growing numbers of Catholics and Jews. Overall, immigration figures rose to their peak in the first decade of the twentieth century.[21]

In 1808, Congress outlawed the African slave trade, but widespread smuggling continued until the Civil War. One of the last examples known was an enterprise organized by a prominent resident of Savannah with collaborators from both north and south. In 1858 the slave ship the *Wanderer* landed about 400 slaves on Jekyll Island. Some of the survivors lived on well into the twentieth century.[22]

Statistics of the slave trade, legal and illegal, are at best the product of informed guesswork, like most figures on immigration, especially before national record-keeping began in 1820. But it seems clear that the greater part of growth in the black population was the product of natural increase throughout the colonial and national periods of American history. The sugarcane fields of the Caribbean were the most voracious consumers of black slaves, whose life expectancy in this region was about seven years.[23]

The period of low immigration after the American Revolution was the period during which the South was becoming committed to cotton. The crop was grown only for domestic use in the colonial period, but around 1786 the sea island variety began to be grown commercially. In 1793 Eli Whitney's invention of the cotton gin opened the way for growing the upland variety, whose green seeds had clung to the lint too stubbornly for it to previously be a cash crop. Quickly the cotton belt engulfed the lower South, and the growing demand for slaves made slavery's hold all the more tenacious.

Immigrants therefore found the rural South a less attractive place to settle, and few came. According to the census of 1850, only one in twenty of the free population, or 5 percent, were of foreign birth; outside the South the numbers were one in seven, or 14 percent. Only one large concentration of foreign born developed in the rural South—the German population in the Texas countryside around San Antonio, Fredericksburg, and New Braunfels. Largely refugees from the liberal revolutions that swept Europe in 1848, these people tended to value liberty and oppose slavery. In large numbers they opposed the Confederacy and joined the Republicans, the party of emancipation.[24]

The other concentrations of foreign born were for the most part in the cities.[25] The white immigrant population of northern cities was slightly higher than that of southern cities, but by 1860, the gap had almost vanished. The foreign share was 39.2 percent in the southern cities and 39.9 percent in northern cities. Southern cities had larger concentrations of foreign-language groups, such as French, Spanish, Italians, and Germans. The immigrants in northern cities were chiefly English-speaking groups, mainly British, Irish, and Canadian in origin. Free blacks also tended to concentrate in the cities, as did northerners who moved South.[26]

The free blacks were nearly all workers, skilled and unskilled. The northern newcomers and the foreign-born, on the other hand, were largely business and professional people, but a substantial number of them were urban workmen who were often in competition with black workers.[27]

The cosmopolitan character of antebellum southern cities is one feature of the Old South that has only recently become visible. The myths of the Old South were the myths of the rural South whether they represented the plantation tradition of the Sunny South or the abolitionist image of the Benighted South.

After the American Revolution, nevertheless, the South at large became distinctive in the homogeneity of its population. Southerners, white and black, became (and still are) overwhelmingly native-born Americans. In the words of historian Rowland T. Berthoff, they were "ethnically more homogeneous than the mixed northern population. Colonial Huguenots, Scots, and Germans having long since been absorbed and their distinctiveness forgotten."[28]

Since immigrants were rare in most of the rural South, the region was not in the forefront of nativist hostility toward immigrants. Still, a number of voters were drawn into the nativist and anti-Catholic American, or Know-Nothing, Party in the 1850s. Its rise in part reflected the decline of the Whig Party, and the new party served former Whigs as another way to oppose the Democrats. In Louisiana, for instance, the American Party was strong in the Catholic sugar parishes that favored protective tariffs and among New Orleans Creoles who used the party as a weapon against Irish newcomers. But the party quickly vanished, consumed in the slavery controversy.[29]

After the Civil War the South went through a time when state and private efforts sought to promote foreign and northern immigration, partly out of a belief that blacks would be lazy workers once released from slavery and partly to increase the white population and thus white control. The efforts, however, had only spotty results.[30] One unusual effect of promoting immigration was the coming of about a thousand Chinese to the Delta section of Mississippi in the mid-1870s—the first sizable Asian population in the South, many of whose descendants are still there.[31]

The effort to promote immigration had such meager results that after the turn of the century, white southerners increasingly shared the opinion of other Americans that the time had come to close the gates. After all, was not the South derived from the best stock, the biggest WASP nest this side of the Atlantic, and therefore the most American of all regions, the salvation of America?

Two well-known incidents of violence, and by no means the only ones, underlined the growing nativism. In 1891 a New Orleans mob hanged or shot eleven Italians suspected of the murder of a local policeman. Six of the Italians had already been acquitted of the crime. In 1915 a Georgia mob spirited from a state prison farm and hanged Leo Frank, falsely accused of murdering a teenage girl in his pencil factory and actually the victim of anti-Semitic bigotry. Two months later a group in white robes climbed Stone Mountain near Atlanta to proclaim the resurrection of the Ku Klux Klan. The Klan's new task was to protect its version of the American way of life not only from blacks, but also from Catholics, Jews, and immigrants in general. In going nativist it also went national, unlike the Reconstruction Klan.[32]

Perhaps, ironically, in ways unseen by the zealots of "Americanism," it was less in some mythical racial "purity" than in the diversity of their backgrounds that southerners were the most American. Despite the melting pots that had bubbled away for two centuries, major elements of the colonial population remained visible in the white, black, Indian, and Hispanic elements of the twentieth-century South.

Striking evidence of diversity can be found in a map published a few years ago in *American Demographics.* Two geographers studied the 1980 census of all 3100 counties in the United States with attention to the presence of five broadly defined ethnic groups: whites, blacks, Hispanics, American Indians, and Asians and Pacific Islanders, all based on people's self-identification. The compilers developed a statistical index to measure each county's relative diversity and ranked them from highest to lowest. The nearest approach to perfection in this regard was San Francisco.[33]

On the map the colors shade off from white to gray to blue, the last representing the greatest diversity. Generally, the farther south one looks on the map the greater

19

the diversity. Blacks in the Southeast and Indians and Hispanics in the Southwest account for much of this, but the presence of the Lumbee Indians helped make Robeson County, North Carolina, the sixth most diverse county in the country—and the most diverse outside of San Francisco, Los Angeles, and New York City. Altogether, six counties in the South appear in the top thirty: two in North Carolina, two in Texas, one in Florida, and one in Georgia.[34]

In 1928 historian Ulrich B. Phillips set forth as the central theme of southern history a determination that the South should be "a white man's country."[35] But he clearly had reference to power, not to population. Where the population was mainly white, little determination would be called for. And if one wants to find a white man's country on the map just described, one must look not at the southernmost rim of the United States but at the northernmost rim, from northern New England westward into Montana, and dipping down as far as Missouri and Nebraska west of the Mississippi River.

2
Ethnic
Southerners

With the waning of ethnic memories after Independence, historical writings on ethnic groups came to resemble historical writings on counties. Both ran to quaint storehouses of dusty antiquities. As for me, I approached the subject by the back door, so to speak, when I was called upon to give a presidential address to the Southern Historical Association twenty years ago. In casting about for a timely topic I hit upon the growing fashion of the "new ethnicity" in the early 1970s.[1]

It had slowly dawned on me that southerners, white and black, were outsiders in much the same way as were recent immigrants. Southerners differed from immigrants, however, in being home-grown outsiders in the nation. Sociologists Lewis Killian and John Shelton Reed had made the ethnic analogy in books then recent, and in 1938, in the process of rediscovering the South, Jonathan Daniels had written that "being a Southerner is like being a Jew. And, indeed, perhaps more needs to be written about the similarity of the minds and emotions of the Jew, the Irishman, the Southerner, and, perhaps, the Pole, as a basis for the better understanding of each of them and of them all."[2]

If there had been any place where the American melting pot worked it was in the South, where two melting pots, white and black, bubbled away side by side, with some of the ingredients spilling over from one into the other. "However surprising it may sound at first," I said back in 1973, "the function of melting pots is to create new ethnic groups. Everybody has a melting pot in his past." Thus what in the colonial period may have been the most diverse population in America had fused into a new ethnic group—or rather two ethnic groups, black and white, that had much in common, however reluctant they were to acknowledge kinship.[3]

Southerners black and white who have moved out of the South, like people who have moved out of other countries, have taken the ethnic culture of the region into black and hillbilly ghettoes—northerners persist in calling all white southerners "hillbillies." Similarly, the exodus of "Okies" to California during the Great Depression has left a firm imprint of southern culture on that state, particularly on the central valley. Bakersfield and Fresno, for instance, are virtually southern towns.[4]

Although the word regionalism came into common usage only in the twentieth century, the phenomenon was a fact of American society almost from its beginnings. The varied cultures of pre-Columbian Indians reflected it. Fairly early in the years of the English colonies, four distinctive regions came to be recognized: the South, New England, the Middle Colonies, and the Backcountry. The regions were distinct partly because geography dictated different economies and societies but also because they were peopled by emigrants from different areas of England and Europe or by greater or lesser numbers from Africa.

Geographically the southern colonies at first had an advantage in climate. They could grow exotic staples unsuited to northern latitudes and prized by the mother country: certain varieties of tobacco around the Chesapeake, rice and indigo farther south.

By the end of the colonial period a North and South had also come to be recognized, variously divided at the Mason-Dixon line (named for the surveyors of the Maryland-Pennsylvania boundary) or at the Potomac River. In 1785 Thomas Jefferson pointed out to the Marquis de Chastellux some differences between the two peoples that sound remarkably contemporary:[5]

In the North they are	In the South they are
cool	fiery
sober	voluptuary
laborious	indolent
independent	unsteady
jealous of their own liberties, and just to those of others	zealous for their own liberties, but trammeling on those of others
interested	generous
chicaning	candid
superstitious and hypocritical in their religion	without attachment or pretention in matters of the heart

Throughout the nineteenth century in the sectional controversies that led to the Civil War, the vision grew of differences between North and South. The connection between region and ethnicity, however, has rarely been acknowledged until recently. As a theoretical construct, regionalism had its heyday in the United States in the years between 1920 and 1950. Regional sensibility ran strongest in literary, artistic, and academic circles, mainly in the West and the South. Such names as Mary Austin, Willa Cather, Ole Rölvaag, Mari Sandoz, Lynn Riggs, George O'Keeffe, Thomas Hart Benton, Benjamin Botkin, William Faulkner, John Crowe Ransom, and Thomas Wolfe suggest the varied uses of regional themes in the arts.

Efforts to develop a rationale for regionalism were led by planners and philosophers of planning like Lewis Mumford, Benton MacKaye, Constance Rourke, and regionalism in a broader sense was promoted by historian Frederick Jackson Turner at the University of Wisconsin, by the literary group in Nashville known first as the Fugitive poets and then as the Vanderbilt Agrarians, and by the Regionalists in Chapel Hill who followed sociologist Howard W. Odum at the University of North Carolina.[6]

During this time, two new and disparate views of southern life began to arise: Agrarianism and Regionalism, the first centered at Vanderbilt University in Nashville and the second at the University of North Carolina at Chapel Hill. The Vanderbilt Agrarians were the first to perfect their arguments. Their manifesto, *I'll Take My Stand*, appeared in 1930. In reaction against both the progressive New South and the image of the benighted

South, the Agrarians championed a traditional society that was religious, more rural than urban, and politically conservative—a society in which human needs were met by family, clanship, folkways, custom, and community. In classic sociological terms, *Gemeinschaft.*

Of course, in the end their agrarianism proved less important as a socio-economic force than as a context for creative literature. The central figures in the movement were the Fugitive poets John Crowe Ransom, Donald Davidson, Allen Tate, and Robert Penn Warren. But, as Louis D. Rubin, Jr. has written, their image of an agrarian South provided "a rich, complex metaphor through which they presented a critique of the modern world. In contrast to the hurried, nervous life of cities, the image of the agrarian South was of a life in which human beings existed serenely and harmoniously." Their critique of the modern frenzy "has since been echoed by commentator after commentator."[7]

In 1893 Frederick Jackson Turner took a new tack in understanding American development in what is probably still the most widely-known single essay by an American historian, "The Significance of the Frontier to American History." After the 1890 population count the superintendent of the census had noted that he could no longer locate a continuous frontier line beyond which population thinned out to fewer than two per square mile. "The existence of an area of free land," Turner wrote, "its continuous recession and the advance of American settlement westward, explain American development." The frontier had shaped the national character in striking ways. Yet in 1893 Turner said, "Four hundred years from the discovery of America, at the end of a hundred years under the Constitution, the frontier has gone and with its going has closed the first period of American history."[8]

With the frontier gone as an active force in American history, Turner cast about for some other unifying concept of American history. He found it in the development of sectionalism, which seemed to him a permanent characteristic of the American scene firmly based on experience and on differing interests that could be projected into the future. At the University of Wisconsin shortly after the turn of the century, Turner instituted courses in the regional history of the American West, the South, and New England.

In 1925 he summed up his ideas in an essay, "The Significance of the Section in American History." That sectionalism was not dying away, he asserted, would be clear enough from reading the newspapers and the debates in Congress, not to speak of analyzing votes in that body. Much of the congressional legislation resembled treaties negotiated between sovereign nations. "The significance of the section in American history," Turner wrote, "is that it is the faint image of a European nation and that we need to reexamine our history in the light of this fact. Our politics and our society have been shaped by the sectional complexity and interplay not unlike what goes on between European nations."[9]

Turner's essay on sections, which focused on the West, offered a basis in history for the Regionalism focusing on the South that Howard Odum was then developing at the University of North Carolina. Odum's protégé and colleague Rupert B. Vance produced the first major work of the regional school in a social history of the cotton complex, *Human Factors in Cotton Culture* (1929), which was a view of an economic and social system on the verge of collapse. Three years later Vance's *Human Geography of the South* (1932) presented an overview of the South at the time, based largely on the 1930 census. There Vance set forth in some detail the "eclectic tasks" of a new Regionalism which would look to "both orderly industrial development and agricultural reform." Research and planning would be the key to a material and cultural renaissance of the South.[10]

Meanwhile, Odum himself had published *An American Epoch* (1930). The book grew from a creative insight that pictured the evolution of southern folk through four generations with a skill few historians could muster. In 1936 he published his magnum opus, *Southern Regions of the United States.* Its title derived from Odum's division of the United States into six regions on the basis of several hundred social, cultural, and economic indices.[11]

Odum preferred the word *regional* to *sectional,* a word too long associated in his mind with conflict. Regionalism was the thing that would exorcise the evil spirits of sectionalism. It would seek to ameliorate conflict and integrate the region into the nation, accepting differences and encouraging diversity in the context of the overall welfare.

Regionalism was more than an attack on sectionalism, of course. It was a concept with implications in literature, geography, history, ecology, anthropology, psychology, economics, political science, and sociology. Regionalism was a means toward synthesis of all the social sciences and, to some extent, of the humanities.

The Odumesque version of Regionalism was, however, too divorced from the mainstream of sociological thought (or from political reality) to survive, except marginally, even in the department that Odum founded. And unlike Henry Grady, whose classic speech "The New South" in 1886 held before his fellow southerners a vision that became a motivating force in history, Odum hardly proved to be the prophet of a post–New South. His vision, in fact, built solidly on Grady's New South creed of economic development. After all, were not most of the region's problems rooted ultimately in poverty?

In Odum's mind regionalism was more than an academic exercise. It was a practical basis on which to pursue social planning. Fundamentally, southern Regionalism was a concept of the "Problem South," which Franklin D. Roosevelt labeled "The Nation's Economic Problem No. 1." He saw the South as a region with shortcomings but also with potentialities that called for constructive attention and the application of rational planning.

Odum held to the idea, widely unfashionable then as

now, that academic research might be "research in service to society," as Guy and Guion Johnson term it in their survey of the first fifty years of Odum's Institute for Research in the Social Sciences.[12] Through the disciples of Odum, as well as agencies of the New Deal, the vision of Regionalism inspired a flood of social science monographs and programs for reform and development.

In the end, however, Odum's chief contribution was that he, like the Agrarians, supplied the impetus of an idea. Agrarianism quickened a generation of southern writers with its vision of tradition beset by change, which became the central theme of the Southern Renaissance in literature just a hundred years after the flowering of New England. Regionalism quickened a generation of social scientists with its vision of the "problem South."

Among the diversified groups in the field, the New Deal state planning boards offered a fleeting promise of regional planning, but most of them evolved into "industry-hunting" boards, in effect official chambers of commerce. A National Resources Planning Board for a time suggested development along the lines endorsed by Odum, but the focus on regionalism faded rapidly as inward-looking Americans found their attention drawn out to Munich, Poland, China, and Pearl Harbor. The NRPB expired in 1943, a casualty of World War II and a conservative reaction against the New Deal.

After the death of Odum in 1954 Regionalism virtually vanished for several decades. Odum's colleague Rupert Vance observed: "Many of the pertinent demands of the regional movement of the thirties have evaporated. The New Deal has been dealt; what is the fighting all about? As the affluent society crosses the Mason-Dixon line, the regionalist of the 1930s turns up as just another 'liberal without a cause.' " [13]

But Regionalism, like Fundamentalism (otherwise a very different phenomenon), proved to be not dead but dormant, and it continued to stir below the surface of popular awareness. It was with folk culture that Odum began and ended his study of regional sociology, initially by studying black folk songs and folk culture and finally by attempting to develop a sociological theory of regional folk culture. When interest in regionalism began to stir once again, its focus was on regional cultures in both the anthropological and the aesthetic sense.

The rebirth of regionalist ideas paralleled a rising interest in ethnicity. In *Outlines of a Philosophy of the History of Man* (1784–1791), the eighteenth-century German romantic Johann Gottfried Herder asserted that each national or ethnic group had a distinctive *Volksgeist* (literally, a spirit of the people, a cultural life derived and experienced from a shared heritage of geography) and that the diversity of such cultures enriched the world. A similar belief sustained Odum's Regionalism. [14] In world history since Herder's time, such national and ethnic cultures have exhibited a dogged resistance to influences which might be expected to work toward more unified cultures. Had not Turner himself said that the section was the faint image of the European nation?

In the absence of a common American culture, the adaptation of immigrants to the available regional culture has been a common experience. In 1973 cultural geographer Wilbur Zelinsky referred to the "Doctrine of the First Effective Settlement." This was his theory that the first European or native white American population had a decisive and persistent effect on later patterns of culture even though the population became more diverse as New England evolved from English Puritan to Irish and Italian Catholic or as the South evolved toward a heavily black slave society.[15]

Several ambitious projects to study the peopling of North America are now in progress, each having produced the first of several volumes: Bernard Bailyn's *The Peopling of British North America;* Donald W. Meinig's *The Shaping of America: A Geographical Perspective on 500 Years of History;* and David Hackett Fischer's *America, A Cultural History,* the first volume of which is entitled *Albion's Seed: Four British Folkways in America.*[16]

In *Albion's Seed,* Fischer applied the idea of Zelinsky's "Doctrine of the First Effective Settlement." Fischer argued that the great majority of the earliest settlers in British America came from the British Isles, called Albion by ancient Greeks and Romans. Whether English, Scottish, Irish, Welsh, or Cornish, nearly all except the Highland Scots spoke English.

Fischer identified four mass migrations from distinct regions of Britain to distinct regions of colonial America. The Great Migration to Massachusetts Bay (about 1629–

1640) was comprised mainly of Puritans from East Anglia, the eastern counties of England. A generation later (1640–1675), tidewater Virginia had an influx of Royalist Cavaliers and their indentured servants from southern England. Largely the younger sons of aristocratic families who had entered commerce, they set the tone for the colony. The Delaware Valley was colonized (about 1675–1725) by Quakers and their sympathizers from the north Midlands of England and from Wales. Later arrivals were European pietists, actively recruited by the Quakers. Finally, the southern backcountry was settled (about 1717–1775) by people who came, if not from Germany, then largely from the Celtic fringe of Scotland, Ireland, Wales, Cornwall, and from England's six northern counties where border battles and migrations had molded the character of the people in common ways. Collectively they were called "borderers." Fischer, however, does not ignore further complexities such as the distinctive coastal culture of South Carolina, with founding families of English from Barbados, Huguenots from France, emigrants from tidewater Virginia, and a majority of black slaves from earlier settlement.

Two historians, Grady McWhiney and Forrest McDonald, have for some years developed a thesis that the borderers developed Celtic ways into the dominant southern culture pattern. Down through the first half of the nineteenth century, they argue, the South remained a thinly populated area of forests and grazing lands. "Such a region was ideally suited for the clannish, herding, leisure-loving Celts, who relished whiskey, gambling, and combat, and who despised hard work, anything English, most government, fences, and any other restraints upon them and their free-ranging livestock."[17]

It was long assumed that the demands of the frontier cut the cords which tied settlers to their homelands. In the late eighteenth century, long before the term "melting pot" became current, J. Hector St. John de Crèvecoeur, a French settler in New York colony said that "individuals of all races of men are melted into a new race." In answer to his own question—"What then is the American, this new man?"—Crèvecoeur answered, "He is either a European or the descendant of an European, hence that strange mixture of blood. . . . I could point out to you a family whose grandfather was an Englishman, whose wife was Dutch, whose son married an French woman, and whose present four sons have now four wives of different nations."[18]

Had it occurred to Crèvecoeur, who had visited the South, he might just as well have written: "He is either an African or the descendant of an African. . . . I could point out to you a man whose grandfather was a Senegambian, whose wife was Angolan, whose son married a Yoruba woman, and whose present four sons have now four wives of different nations."

But for all the transformative effects of the New World, the disparate British ways of life persisted. Most British settlers spoke a common language, but they carried with them different cultural attitudes from their home regions to their new regions. They spoke different dialects, favored different foods, named and raised their children differently, built their houses in different styles, engaged in different games and recreations, and organized their societies differently. In short, they transformed British regionalism into American regionalism.

This left a permanent mark on the country. People in the South favored fried foods in part because their ancestors in southern and western England did. And hill-billies who distilled bug juice up in the mountain coves did so because their ancestors produced usquebaugh in northern Britain. They pronounced *where* as *whar* and *there* as *thar* because that was common to the Scottish and Irish borderlands. Terms like *hoosier, redneck,* and *cracker* also derived from the borderlands. The drawl associated with Virginia cavaliers replicates a dialect common in southern and western England. But the legacy goes well beyond language to gender relations, religious practices, propensities to violence (common to the borderlands and to the South), and other characteristics. Cultural continuity however, is not unique to people of British origin. Degrees of it can be found among descendants of settlers from any country.

Fischer, in the conclusion to *Albion's Seed,* sketched out his plan for future volumes of his cultural history in which he expected to pursue further the connections between ethnic and regional patterns. The seven regional cultures he postulated are, I think, not now part of the mental maps most Americans have of their country.

North-South antipathies that appeared long before the Civil War still remain strong, at least strong enough to be a staple of American humor. During World War II, for example, there was an incident both funny and sad (and probably apocryphal) of three German prisoners of war who escaped into the Tennessee mountains, where they stopped for a drink of water. A mountain granny told them to "git," and when they ignored her, she shot them dead. When the sheriff scolded her for shooting desperate prisoners, she burst into tears. She would not have shot them if she had known they were Germans. The sheriff demanded to know what in tarnation she thought she was shooting at. "Why," she said, "I thought they was Yankees." [19]

Complexities abound in the westward migration of the colonial cultures and in the new ethnic cultures that entered the scene. The growing ethnic pluralism of the United States after 1820, Fischer contends, did not diminish regional identities but rather enhanced and at the same time complicated them. New immigrants, Fischer notes, "did not assimilate American culture in general. They tended to adopt the folkways of the regions in which they settled." [20] Instead of one American melting pot, there were many.

Fischer's book is challenging, but it has not been immune to criticism. In 1991 the *William and Mary Quarterly* devoted a large section to several critiques. The *Quar-*

terly called it a Forum, but Fischer said it seemed to him "more like what happened in the Colosseum."[21] Fischer's work, nevertheless, strongly suggests that Regionalism has been not dead but dormant—or neither. Perhaps it has simply been unnoticed by the literati.

3
Southern
Ethnics

It now seems likely that the twentieth century, which began with a record decade of immigration, will end with another in the 1990s. In fact, if one could count undocumented immigrants, a new record may have been set in the 1980s. During the decade 1981–1990 legal immigrants numbered 7.3 million, just 1.4 million short of the 8.7 million who came in 1901–1910.[1]

In the 1920s the National Origins Laws closed the "Golden Door" to America to all but a trickle of immigrants. The quotas set then favored the oldest European stock but still left the gates open to newcomers from the Americas. In the 1920s the Hispanic population became the fastest growing minority in the country—chiefly due to Mexicans drawn to farm labor in the Southwest—only to face rising hostility during the Depression and the illegal repatriation of about 400,000 immigrants by local governments.[2]

In the late 1930s the exclusionary laws remained unchanged. The plight of refugees from dictatorship and war was acknowledged chiefly in President Roosevelt's directive that the consular service grant them "the most humane and favorable treatment under the law."

After World War II resistance to change persisted. President Truman proposed favorable treatment for displaced persons in Europe, but action came slowly. Congress did pass a War Brides Act in 1945 but still banned Asian brides until 1947. Not until 1948 did the Displaced Persons Act open special quotas for refugees. This would be renewed by a Refugee Relief Act in 1953.[3]

It would be excessive to detail actions on special cases, but four major postwar changes in the laws call for brief notice: the Immigration Act of 1952, better known as the McCarran-Walter Act, and the Immigration Acts of 1965, 1986, and 1990.[4]

The McCarran-Walter Act preserved the national origins quotas of the 1920s and enacted harsh restraints against suspected Communists, but the law also opened small quotas for Asians and gave the attorney general a "parole power" to admit refugees otherwise ineligible. (A later Refugee Act of 1980 opened the door to people who could show a "well-founded fear of persecution.")[5]

The Immigration Act of 1965, Lyndon Johnson said, corrected "a cruel and enduring wrong in the conduct of the American nation."[6] It ended the national origins quotas, but it retained a ceiling on the total number admitted and set a maximum of 20,000 from any one country, with strong preference for close relatives of citizens and resident aliens and a lesser preference for those with certain skills and talents. Such provisions at first favored immigrants from Europe, as expected, but before long they fostered a "chain immigration" of Asians and Hispanics bringing in relatives, each of whom could then usher in more.[7]

All along, however, there had been a flow of illegal

aliens across the land borders and shorelines. Finally in 1986 the Congress decided to declare an amnesty and permanent residence for all who had been resident since before 1982. In addition to that, if the government decided there was a shortage of farm labor, more aliens could come in with temporary visas and become permanent residents after two more years—if they had worked in the United States ninety days in each of those three years. Clearly a demand for cheap labor still drove much of the immigration policy.[8]

The Immigration Act of 1990 continued that practice and enlarged the legal total of immigrants from 490,000 to 700,000. A majority of these (490,000) would have to be relatives of people already here, but 140,000 would be skilled workers, 55,000 would be from nations neglected in previous quotas, and 10,000 would be people ready to invest $1 million or more. The inscription on the Statue of Liberty, a news article stated, should be changed from "Give me your tired, your poor, your huddled masses. . ." to "Give me your skilled, your rich, your lucky. . . ."[9]

The post–World War II immigrants are coming from different origins than previously, and they are going to different destinations, more than ever to the West and the South and changing a pattern that had prevailed for nearly two centuries after the 1770s.

Like most others I only slowly gathered, from observation more than from systematic evidence, what was happening. For example, universities in the Durham–

Raleigh–Chapel Hill Triangle have long harbored a more diverse community than most of the surrounding region, so the changes there were less startling than in other places. As one frequent visitor from Japan described it, "The Raleigh–Durham–Chapel Hill area is a microcosm of American politics. In the political arena, very liberal Democrats compete with very conservative Republicans. . . . The area offers a startling contrast between traditional and post-industrial America. Vestiges of the ante-bellum Southern aristocracy exist beside high-technology industries. Here the foreigner can observe 'red-necks' as well as 'Yuppies.' Here is a window into both America's past and its future." [10]

The first sign of a new and fruitful relationship came in the fall of 1968 when I returned from a Fulbright professorship in Vienna to find a Japanese professor of American history in my seminar. Six years later another appeared, and since 1974 there has been almost a yearly visit of one or more Japanese professors or students pursuing southern history or literature.

The population of this area has become more diverse with the growth of the Research Triangle Park (founded in 1955)—the name signifying the three major universities in the area. [11] The Park, however, has not been the only destination of immigrants to North Carolina. So many Vietnamese refugees gravitated to Fort Bragg and Pope Air Force base that the nearby town of Fayetteville got the new name of "Fayettenam." One Mexican student in Chapel Hill recently engaged in a research project of interviewing Mexican women in a North Carolina county where numbers of Mexicans (many of them illegal immigrants) have been recruited to work in hosiery mills—in the "rent-a-slave" program, as some locals called it.[12] Many of these immigrants, of course, have been farm laborers.

Not everybody found the population growth in the Triangle an unmixed blessing. It ran prices up and brought crowding, traffic jams, and a much busier and noisier airport. But the growing population also brought a new diversity to the culture and the cuisine of the triangle, where one could easily find restaurants specializing in Chinese, Japanese, Vietnamese, French, Italian, Indian, Eastern European, Moroccan, and Mexican dishes. Down-home cooking did not vanish, however. It flourished, to some degree, as an exotic treat for newcomers. One Chapel Hill restaurant invited them to "Put a little South in your mouth."

Foreign investment is all over the Southeast, not just in the Triangle. The book *Power Shift* (1975) by Kirkpatrick Sale, which popularized the term Sunbelt, was quickly translated into Japanese and seems to explain Japanese interest in the region for investment in recent years.[13] Much of the foreign investment is also European: British, German, French, Dutch, Italian, and Swiss. Conspicuous examples may be found along the route between my home in North Carolina and my birthplace in upstate South Carolina.

This is the belt that newsman Jonathan Daniels, in his

book *A Southerner Discovers the South* (1938), called "Gold Avenue" because of the wealth derived from the textile mills that had sprung up along the route of the Southern Railway. The same belt is now traversed by I-85, sometimes called the *Strassenbahn*, and is seeing "a collision of culture that economists say is one version of the future." They might better have said of the present.[14]

A BMW assembly plant at Greer, South Carolina, will be the next and no doubt biggest along that stretch. Michelin's North American headquarters is already there, along with industries that make "everything from soccer balls (Umbro) to toner for fax machines (Mita) to ball-point pens (Bic) to fibers (Hoechst)." Greenville, South Carolina, has a private French-language school. Spartanburg used to have one of the best German delicatessens around. It has now been replaced by a Mexican restaurant, perhaps a sign of the times.

The new distribution of newcomers has been dramatic. The southern states as defined by the census included in their 1940 population only 5.47 percent of all foreign born in the United States, approximately the same as in 1900. As late as 1960, the South accounted for only 9 percent of the total foreign born, but by 1990 the South's share had risen to 23.2 percent. That share of foreign born, however, was still not in even ratio with the region's share of total population, 34.4 percent. Within the South, the foreign born still accounted for only 5 percent of the regional population, well short of their 7.9 percent of the national population; that, in turn, is little more than half the 14.6 percent of foreign born in 1910 on the eve of World War I.[15]

Not all new ethnics, however, come from abroad. The South, long a seedbed of population for the nation, has also seen a reversal in that pattern. More people, both native and foreign, have moved into the region than out of it in the last three decades.

One of the fast growing new ethnic groups is, in fact, northerners. During the 1970s the Northeast lost 700,000 and the Midwest another 700,000 people while the South gained 2.6 million and the West 1.4 million. The trend continued in the 1980s when the Northeast lost 297,000 and the Midwest 116,000 while the South gained 1.4 million and the West 964,000 domestic migrants.[16] Since the mid-1960s, moreover, the South has had a net gain in the migration of blacks with more entering or reentering the South than leaving.[17]

Of course, the newcomers have had more impact in some places than in others. The heaviest concentrations of Hispanic population within the South are along the southernmost rim. In 1990 newcomers in Texas numbered 3.5 million and in Florida 1.5, but six more states numbered at least 100,000 each: Louisiana, Alabama, Georgia, North Carolina, Virginia, and Maryland.

Asian migration followed similar patterns. A number of Vietnamese were drawn to Versailles, Louisiana, which became maybe the most intensely Vietnamese community in the country (if not the largest) and represented a portion of the nearly 12,000 Asians who had settled around greater New Orleans because they were drawn to a congenial climate not unlike Southeast Asia's.[18] Versailles residents were in effect drawn from three fishing villages southeast of Saigon from which most of them came. In 1988, about 40 percent of them already owned their own homes, but the newcomers had trouble with biased neighbors. Several got death threats amid rumors that missing pets had gone into Vietnamese stewpots. Another complaint, more likely based on fact, was about the pungent fish they hung out to dry.

There is a fast growing literature on the newest immigration to the South. Most of it is in scattered articles, but some has been gathered in books. In 1988 one group of historians published a collection of essays which surveyed important aspects of the new developments, and the volume contains useful footnotes and a bibliographic essay that make it an essential starting place for study of the subject. Edited by Randall M. Miller and George E. Pozzetta, the volume has an inspired title, *Shades of the Sunbelt,* linked to a more pedestrian subtitle, *Essays on Ethnicity, Race, and the Urban South.*[19]

One limitation of the book, or perhaps its strength, is its emphasis on Florida. It avoids obsession with Miami although it includes an excellent piece by Raymond Mohl on the "ethnic caldron" of the city's politics. Not that Miami is unimportant, but it is a special case. The city, like much of South Florida, was "America's Last Frontier," a country built and settled in this century by northerners and never really part of the Old or the New

South.[20] Over fifty years ago when Jonathan Daniels set out to write *A Southerner Discovers the South*, he suddenly realized halfway down the peninsula that he had entered Yankee Florida, whereupon he said, he turned around and headed north back into the South.[21]

Since the 1940s Florida has seen successive waves of new immigration. The arrival of Jewish retirees, in such numbers as to give Miami a proportion of Jewish population second only to New York's, is a movement said to be the only mass migration of the elderly in modern times. Then, after Fidel Castro seized power in 1959, Cubans arrived in such numbers as to make Miami into a "Little Havana." The ethnic mixture has been whimsically expressed by hotels that serve up huevos rancheros with lox.

The Cuban presence became the magnet that drew other Latin Americans to Miami, and they established such a network of communications as to make Miami the unofficial cultural capital of Latin America. In 1973 Miami elected a mayor of Puerto Rican background. In 1985 he lost to Cuban-born Xavier Suarez, and Latinos came into control of the city commission and all the major administrative jobs except that of the police chief, who was a recently-appointed black.[22]

The rest of Florida is hardly typical either but is perhaps a harbinger of changes to come. In every decade of the century 1890–1990, the state's percentage of population growth outpaced that of the nation. From being one of the least populated states it went to being the fourth largest. Its population density went from less than a third to more than triple the nation's average; its percentage of urban population from less than half to nearly ten percentage points above the nation's average; its percentage of people aged sixty-five or over from slightly less to well above the nation's average; and its percentage foreign-born went from less than a third to nearly twice the nation's average. In 1990 these foreign-born made up over 14.5 percent of Florida's population.[23]

Just over half the foreign-born were Hispanic (mostly Cuban), but there was a great variety of other ethnic groups. At one place or another in Florida one can hear almost any European language including both Canadian and Caribbean versions of French and such rarities as Finnish and Romanian. Asians numbered only a little over 3 percent of the foreign-born, but they were mostly among the very recently arrived.

One cannot easily generalize about the South's Latino population at large. It includes numbers of Puerto Ricans who, as citizens, are not counted as immigrants. Hispanics include Tejanos whose roots in the land go deeper than those of the "Anglos," an established population that, in San Antonio especially, exercised political clout before the turn of the century and now does once again.[24] "We never crossed a border," they say, "the border crossed us."[25] Cuban migrants (along with Asians) have tended to be more middle class and educated than Mexicans or than the native population.

Mexican newcomers have largely been unskilled

workers. World War II renewed growers' interest in
cheap foreign labor. More recently Mexicans have been
joined by refugees from civil war and poverty in Central
America. In the year from May 5, 1987, to May 1, 1988,
however, applicants for amnesty under the Immigration
Act of 1986 were 73.3 percent Mexican. The next largest
group from a single country were Salvadoran (6.5 percent). All but 14.3 percent of the total came from Latin
or Caribbean countries.[26]

Obviously, then, one new frontier for southern historians is the role of ethnic diversity in the region—more
than just that represented by black and white. Ethnically diverse populations have been here all along (if
in limited numbers until recently), as I noted in 1973:
"a few reminders of forgotten Spaniards and French-
men, some Mexican-Americans renamed Chicanos, some
Cuban cigar-makers in Tampa and Ybor City and the
more recent Cuban refugees, some German counties out
in Texas, Cajuns up the bayous, Italians in New Orleans,
Hungarians over in Tangipahoa Parish, a scattering of
Czechs, Dutch, Ukranians, and in Mississippi, even Chinese. Jews are visible, if scarce, in most localities; poli-
ticians in Charleston used to reckon with the Irish and
Germans; and there are those enclaves of mixed-blood
Lumbees, Tuscaroras, 'Brass Ankles,' Melungeons, and
Turks, not to mention remnants of Cherokees, Catawbas,
Creeks, and Seminoles."[27]

What, then, might history suggest we expect from the
growing numbers and variety of domestic and foreign

newcomers? Reactions to migration have an especially strong tendency to repeat themselves. Foremost among these reactions is fear and suspicion of strangers in the land. The dread of cultural conquest seems ingrained, no matter how ill founded. One early southerner, at least, did get it right. Chief Powhatan told Captain John Smith of the many "who do informe me your coming is not for trade, but to invade my people and possesse my country."[28]

But John Smith's successors kept getting it wrong. Benjamin Franklin, for instance, wanted to know, "Why should Pennsylvania, founded by the English, become a colony of Aliens, who will shortly be so numerous as to Germanize us instead of our Anglifying them?"[29] Domestic migrants may be the outsiders as well. On cars around the Triangle area one sees imitation state licenses inscribed "Native" and bumper stickers that say: "We don't care how they do it in New York." Any day we may see graffiti that say: "Yankee Go Home."

In some cases black and white natives have united in their fear of losing jobs and business to newcomers, although others argue that immigrants have added more than they have taken from the economy. By common repute Asian immigrants have been the highest achievers in both enterprise and education. A study of Vietnamese refugees in North Carolina, for instance, shows that employers invariably praise their habits of diligence. This is apparently the result of an ingrained work ethic more Confucian than Protestant in its roots.[30]

While there is a high degree of xenophobia among blacks, on occasion black leaders have made common cause politically with Latinos rather than fight over the crumbs from the table. For the most part, in the South and elsewhere, the foreign-born follow a time-honored habit of voting for the traditional party of "outsiders," the Democrats. Cuban newcomers and refugees from Marxist movements elsewhere, however, have become the great exceptions. These groups have tended toward the Republicans, whom they have perceived as tougher on Communists.

It has been interesting to see southern black political leaders who have been forced to adopt the ethnic political awareness that northern leaders have had for years. Not long ago, then Mayor Andrew Young of Atlanta described the poor veterinary service at the Atlanta Zoo as being like Korean medicine—only to face a storm of protest from a Korean community of about 15,000. It took quick footwork to explain that he had in mind the kind of handicaps American surgeons worked under in the television program M*A*S*H.[31]

Demands for English as an official language parallel the campaign which occurred over a century ago to forbid German-language schools in the Middle West. Miami was the birthplace of the latter-day "English Only" effort. During the 1960s a movement developed there for bilingual education, mainly in transitional programs, and in 1973 the Dade County Commissioners declared the county officially bilingual, which meant some accomodation of Spanish in public services. In 1980 reaction in the "Anglo" community generated a referendum in which the voters approved establishment of English as the only official language for Dade County. A leader in the movement was an immigrant from Russia.

The movement went national that same year as California Senator S. I. Hayakawa introduced an Official English Bill in Congress and founded U. S. English, an organization to promote the cause. During the 1980s the movement fed on nativist sentiments, and a number of states adopted Official English measures, but they seem to have had little other than symbolic effect, and the movement has stalled.[32]

When the North Carolina legislature took up the subject, one of my colleagues wanted to know: "What's the matter with the way we been talkin'?" Many readers have probably heard an older joke: What do you call a person who speaks two languages? Bilingual. What do you call a person who speaks three languages? Trilingual. What do you call a person who speaks one language? American. Some groups such as Greek-Americans, however, have assimilated without ditching the old culture by sending their children both to public and to parochial schools where they learn the Greek language. On the other hand, they have never sought, as some Latinos have, to make bilingualism an official requirement.

The most likely outcome will be an old pattern described years ago by historian Marcus Lee Hansen: second-generation Americans reject the old language and culture in order to be accepted as American, and the third generation desperately tries to recover its heritage. Hansen called it "the almost universal phenomenon that what the son wishes to forget the grandson wishes to remember." Hansen even cited *Gone With the Wind* as an example of the third-generation phenomenon, written by a granddaughter of the Confederacy.[33]

But that phenomenon reaches far beyond the third generation. American Indians, the oldest immigrant group, keep reaching for their roots. One recent example is the Takawana family of Ft. Smith, Arkansas, full-blooded Comanches who keep in touch with Comanche tradition and tribal politics. But Cliff, the husband, has a business degree and directs the Boy Scouts in northwest Arkansas. His wife Cheryl Ann supervises a program to teach English to Vietnamese refugees. Such renewed ethnic pride has meaning for the South, since three of the ten states with the largest Indian populations are southern: Oklahoma has the largest of all, North Carolina ranks seventh, and Texas eighth.[34]

Experience so far has shown that Americans want to keep chucking out the rich feast of languages that immigrants bring in, along with those languages the earliest inhabitants invented. Much evidence suggests that immigrants need no special prodding to learn English—it comes naturally to the second generation—but it tends to come along with a rejection of the old tongue. For instance, Haitians in Miami seem particularly insistent on learning English. Some 40 percent of those who read newspapers said they read the *Miami Herald* rather than French or Creole papers.

Little research has been done on the group as yet, but in various ways they differ from the stereotype. They have achieved an average of 7.6 years of schooling—coming from a country in which 80 percent have no schooling at all—and most attempt further schooling. More than half sought additional education in the United States. They are at least semi-skilled; few come from the farm.

A study by the Hispanic Policy Development Project showed that in 1986 already 42.7 percent of Hispanics were bilingual and preferred English, and 55.9 percent of those under twenty years old preferred English. In fact English was already the mother tongue—the first language learned—of 30 percent of Hispanics.[35]

My colleague, anthropologist James L. Peacock III, has remarked on how quickly quite diverse ethnic groups have assimilated not only English but southern accents. Students from Korea and India, for instance, who spent their teenage years in small North Carolina towns talk like natives of the same places. The phenomenon of assimilation to regional patterns has long been noted on the part of ethnic groups with deeper roots in the South. Moreover, to change is not necessarily to lose a distinctive identity but is often to enrich it through syncretic combinations, such as Jewish southerners whose roots go back into the colonial era, or Afro-Catholics, or Japanese war brides whose world view has been found to combine southern evangelical and Japanese Buddhist themes.[36] Living cultures do not resist change forever.

All along, a few historians have been paying attention to the elements of ethnic diversity in the South, and in recent years there has been a growing interest. It may be an accident rather than evidence of a trend, but the *Journal of American Ethnic History,* published by the Immigration History Society, is edited in the South at the Georgia Institute of Technology by Ronald H. Bayor, who himself has pursued research on ethnic groups in Atlanta and other southern cities.

Historians of immigration and ethnicity have led the way in the study of southern ethnicity, but historians of the South can no longer assume, as most have done, that the subject is outside their purview. Now, just over 200 years after the birth of the Cotton Belt and 100 years after the birth of the New South, the conviction grows that the region is at a new juncture in its history. One thing seems already clear about the post–New South. The shades of the Sunbelt will no longer be a simple matter of black and white. They will span a much broader spectrum of color.

Notes

Chapter 1: Natives and Newcomers

1. Albert Cowdrey, *This Land, This South* (Lexington: University Press of Kentucky, 1983), 11–28.

2. John M. Blum et al., *The National Experience: A History of the United States*, 4th ed. (New York: Harcourt Brace Jovanovich, 1993), 1.

3. Ella Lonn, *Foreigners in the Confederacy* (Chapel Hill: University of North Carolina Press, 1940), 1.

4. Francis Butler Simkins and Charles P. Roland, *A History of the South*, 4th ed. (New York: Alfred A. Knopf, 1972), 36–37.

5. Peter H. Wood, *Black Majority: Negroes in Colonial South Carolina from 1670 to the Stono Rebellion* (New York: Alfred A. Knopf, 1974), xiv. One historian of the slave trade expressed surprise at how early the slaves' origins ceased to be mentioned in notices of slave sales for seasoned blacks (Elizabeth Donnan, "The Slave Trade into South Carolina Before the American Revolution," *American Historical Review* 33 [July 1928]: 817n). For a different view see Dan C. Littlefield, "'Abundancy of Negroes in that Nation': The Colonial South Carolina," in *The Meaning of South Carolina History: Essays in Honor of George C. Rogers, Jr.*, ed. Daniel R. Chesnutt and Clyde N. Wilson (Columbia: University of South Carolina Press, 1991), 19–38.

Notes

6. Wood, *Black Majority,* esp. pp. 167–94. See also Charles Y. Joyner, *Down by the Riverside: A South Carolina Black Slave Community* (Urbana: University of Illinois Press, 1984); Guy B. Johnson, *Folk Culture on St. Helena Island* (Chapel Hill: University of North Carolina, 1930); Philip D. Curtin, *The Atlantic Slave Trade: A Census* (Madison: University of Wisconsin Press, 1969). On the Gullah tongue, see Lorenzo Dow Turner, *Africanisms in the Gullah Dialect* (Chicago: University of Chicago Press, 1949), 1.

7. David Ramsay, *The History of South Carolina from its First Settlement in 1670 to the Year 1808,* 2 vols. (Charleston, S.C.: David Longworth, 1809), 1: 22–23. In his discussion Ramsay took no notice of black ethnicity.

8. Ibid., 23.

9. Rupert B. Vance, in collaboration with Nadia Danilevsky, *All These People: The Nation's Human Resources in the South* (Chapel Hill: University of North Carolina Press, 1945), 14–18.

10. See Charles Reznikoff, *The Jews of Charleston: A History of an American Jewish Community* (Philadelphia: Jewish Historical Society of America, 1950); and Arthur Henry Hirsch, *The Huguenots of Colonial South Carolina* (Durham, N.C.: Duke University Press, 1928). See also Leonard Dinnerstein and Mary Dale Palsson, eds., *Jews in the South* (Baton Rouge: Louisiana State University, 1973).

11. George Fenwick Jones, *The Georgia Dutch: From the Rhine and Danube to the Savannah, 1733–1783* (Athens: University of Georgia Press, 1992); Amanda Johnson, *Georgia as Colony and State* (1938; reprint, Atlanta, Ga.: Cherokee Publishing Company, 1970); E. Merton Coulter, *A Short History of Georgia* (Chapel Hill: University of North Carolina Press, 1960).

12. See Park Rouse, Jr., *The Great Wagon Road from Philadelphia to the South* (New York: McGraw-Hill, 1973).

13. Frederick Jackson Turner, "The Significance of the Frontier in American History," in *The Frontier in American History* (New York: Henry Holt, 1920), 12.

14. Robert W. Ramsey, *Carolina Cradle: Settlement of the Northwest Carolina Frontier, 1747–1762* (Chapel Hill: University of North Carolina Press, 1964).

15. See Duane Meyer, *The Highland Scots of North Carolina, 1732–1776* (Chapel Hill: University of North Carolina Press, 1961).

16. See Gotthardt Bernheim, *History of German Settlements of North and South Carolina* (Philadelphia: Lutheran Book Store, 1872), and Orlando Benedict Mayer, *The Dutch Fork* (Columbia, S.C.: Dutch Fork Press, 1982).

17. See John Tate Lanning, *The Spanish Missions of Georgia* (Chapel Hill: University of North Carolina Press, 1935); Paul Quattlebaum, *The Land Called Chicora: The Carolinas Under Spanish Rule 1520–1670* (Gainesville: University of Florida Press, 1952).

18. See Carl Brasseaux, *The Founding of New Acadia: The Beginnings of Acadian Life in Louisiana, 1765–1803* (Baton Rouge: Louisiana State University Press, 1987); John H. Dormon, *The People Called Cajun: An Introduction to an Ethnohistory* (Lafayette: Center for Louisiana Studies, University of Southwestern Louisiana, 1983); William Faulkner Rushton, *The Cajuns* (New York: Farrar, Strauss & Giroux, 1979).

19. Population figures from Peter H. Wood, "The Changing Population of the Colonial South: An Overview by Race and Region, 1685–1790," in *Powhatan's Mantle: Indians in the Colonial South*, ed. Peter H. Wood, Gregory A. Waselkov, and M. Thomas Hatley (Lincoln: University of Nebraska Press, 1989), 38–39. For an overview see Charles Hudson, *The Southeastern Indians* (Knoxville: University of Tennessee Press, 1976); Grant

Notes

Foreman, *Indian Removal: The Emigration of the Five Civilized Tribes* (Norman: University of Oklahoma Press, 1966). See also J. Anthony Paredes, *Indians of the Southeastern United States in the Late Twentieth Century* (Tuscaloosa: University of Alabama Press, 1992). There is a sizeable amount of additional literature on Indians of the South.

20. Leonard Dinnerstein, *Ethnic Americans: A History of Immigration,* 3d ed. (New York: Harper and Row, 1988), 16. Overall figures on immigration to the United States from 1820 and their sources are given in George B. Tindall and David E. Shi, *America: A Narrative History,* 3d ed. (New York: W. W. Norton, 1992), A40–A48.

21. Tindall and Shi, *America: A Narrative History,* A44.

22. Tom Henderson Wells, *The Slave Ship Wanderer* (Athens: University of Georgia Press, 1968).

23. See Philip D. Curtin, *The Atlantic Slave Trade.*

24. See Terry G. Jordan, *German Seed in Texas Soil: Immigrant Farmers in Nineteenth Century Texas* (Austin: University of Texas Press, 1966).

25. See Dennis C. Rousey, "Aliens in the Wasp Nest: Ethnocultural Diversity in the Antebellum Urban South," *Journal of American History* 79 (June 1992): 152–64.

26. See Fletcher Melvin Green, *The Role of the Yankee in the Old South,* Mercer University Lamar Lectures, No. 11 (Athens: University of Georgia Press, 1972).

27. For more information, see Ira Berlin and Herbert G. Gutman, "Natives and Immigrants, Freedmen and Slaves: Urban Workingmen in the Antebellum American South," *American Historical Review* 86 (December 1983): 1175–1200; and Randall M. Miller, "The Enemy Within: Some Effects of Foreign Immigrants on Antebellum Southern Cities," *Southern Studies* 24 (Spring 1985): 30–53.

28. Rowland T. Berthoff, "Southern Attitudes Toward Immigration, 1865–1914," *Journal of Southern History* 17 (August 1951): 328–60. Quotation on p. 343.

29. William Darrell Overdyke, *The Know-Nothing Party in the South* (Baton Rouge: Louisiana State University Press, 1950).

30. Walter Lynwood Fleming, "Immigration to the Southern States," *Political Science Quarterly* 20 (January 1905): 276–97; Bert James Loewenberg, "Efforts of the South to Encourage Immigration, 1865–1900," *South Atlantic Quarterly* 33 (October 1934): 363–85; Berthoff, "Southern Attitudes Toward Immigration," 328–60.

31. James W. Loewen, *The Mississippi Chinese: Between Black and White* (Cambridge, Mass.: Harvard University Press, 1971); Robert Seto Quan, *Lotus Among the Magnolias: The Mississippi Chinese* (Jackson: University Press of Mississippi, 1988).

32. Alexander DeConde, *Half Bitter, Half Sweet: An Excursion into Italian-American History* (New York: Scribners, 1971), 121–25; Leonard Dinnerstein, *The Leo Frank Case* (New York: Columbia University Press, 1968); David M. Chalmers, *Hooded Americanism: The History of the Ku Klux Klan* (New York: F. Watts, 1981).

33. James Paul Allen and Eugene James Turner, "Where Diversity Reigns," *American Demographics* 12 (August 1990): 34–38. Map on p. 37. See also Allen and Turner, *We the People: Atlas of American Ethnic Diversity* (New York: Macmillan, 1988).

34. On the Indians of Robeson County, see Gerald M. Sides, *Lumbee Indian Histories: Race, Ethnicity, and Indian Identity in the Southern United States* (New York: Cambridge University Press, 1993).

35. Ulrich B. Phillips, "The Central Theme of Southern History," *American Historical Review* 34 (October 1928): 30–43. Quotation on p. 31.

Chapter 2: Ethnic Southerners

1. George B. Tindall, "Beyond the Mainstream: The Ethnic Southerners," *Journal of Southern History* 40 (February 1974): 3–18. Reprinted in Tindall, *The Ethnic Southerners* (Baton Rouge: Louisiana State University Press, 1976), 1–21. See also Michael Novak, *The Rise of the Unmeltable Ethnics: Politics and Culture in the Seventies* (New York: Macmillan, 1972); Andrew M. Greeley, *Why Can't They Be Like Us* (New York: E. P. Dutton, 1971); Peter Schrag, *The Decline of the WASP* (New York: Simon and Schuster, 1971).

2. Lewis M. Killian, *White Southerners* (New York: Random House, 1970); John S. Reed, *The Enduring South* (Chapel Hill: University of North Carolina Press, 1972); quotation from Jonathan Daniels, *A Southerner Discovers the South* (New York: Macmillan, 1938), 8.

3. George B. Tindall, "Beyond the Mainstream," 3–18. For brief treatments of both groups see Thomas C. Holt, "Afro-Americans," and John Shelton Reed, "Southerners," in *The Harvard Encyclopedia of American Ethnic Groups,* ed. Stephan Thernstrom (Cambridge, Mass.: Belknap Press of Harvard University Press, 1980): 5–23, 944–48.

4. See James Noble Gregory, *An American Exodus: The Dust Bowl Migration and Okie Culture in California* (New York: Oxford University Press, 1989).

5. Thomas Jefferson to the Marquis de Chastellux, September 2, 1785, *The Papers of Thomas Jefferson,* ed. Julian Boyd (Princeton, N.J.: Princeton University Press, 1953), 8: 468.

6. Robert L. Dorman, in *Revolt of the Provinces: The Regionalist Movement in America, 1920–1945* (Chapel Hill: University of North Carolina Press, 1993), surveys these and other

phases of regionalism, especially in literature and planning. See also George B. Tindall, "Regionalism," *Encyclopedia of American Social History,* ed. Mary Cupiec Cayton et al., 3 vols. (New York: Charles Scribner's Sons, 1993), 1: 531–41.

7. Louis D. Rubin, introduction to Twelve Southerners, *I'll Take My Stand: The South and the Agrarian Tradition* (Baton Rouge: Louisiana State University Press, 1977), xxxi.

8. Frederick Jackson Turner, "The Significance of the Frontier in American History," in *The Frontier in American History* (New York: Henry Holt, 1920), 1, 38.

9. Turner, "The Significance of the Section in American History," *Wisconsin Magazine of History* 8 (March 1925), 255–80. Quotation on p. 279.

10. Rupert B. Vance, *Human Factors in Cotton Culture* (Chapel Hill: University of North Carolina Press, 1929), and Vance, *Human Geography of the South* (Chapel Hill: University of North Carolina Press, 1932), 490, 491.

11. Howard W. Odum, *An American Epoch: Southern Portraiture in the National Picture* (New York: Henry Holt, 1930); and Odum, *Southern Regions of the United States* (Chapel Hill: University of North Carolina Press, 1936).

12. See Guy Benton Johnson and Guion Griffis Johnson, *Research in Service to Society: The First Fifty Years of the Institute for Research in Social Science at the University of North Carolina* (Chapel Hill: University of North Carolina Press, 1980).

13. Rupert B. Vance, "The Sociological Implications of Southern Regionalism," *Regionalism and the South: Selected Papers of Rupert Vance,* ed. John Reed and Daniel J. Singal (Chapel Hill: University of North Carolina Press, 1982), 211. Reprinted from *Journal of Southern History* 26 (February 1982): 44–56.

14. Johann Gottfried Herder, *Reflections on the Philosophy of*

Notes

the History of Mankind, trans. Frank E. Manuel (Chicago: University of Chicago Press, 1968; originally published as *Ideen zur Philosophie der Geschichte der Menschheit*). See also Isaiah Berlin, *Vico and Herder: Two Studies in the History of Ideas* (London: Hogarth Press, 1976).

15. Wilbur Zelinsky, *The Cultural Geography of the United States* (Englewood Cliffs, N.J.: Prentice Hall, 1973), 10, 13–14, 34, 81.

16. Bernard Bailyn, *The Peopling of North America: An Introduction* (New York: Knopf, 1986); Bernard Bailyn, with the assistance of Barbara DeWolfe, *Voyagers to the West: A Passage in the Peopling of America on the Eve of the Revolution* (New York: Knopf, 1986); Donald William Meinig, *The Shaping of America: A Geographical Perspective on 500 Years of History* (New Haven, Conn.: Yale University Press, 1986); and David Hackett Fischer, *Albion's Seed: Four British Folkways in America* (New York: Oxford University Press, 1989).

17. See Grady McWhiney, *Cracker Culture: Celtic Ways in the Old South* (Tuscaloosa: University of Alabama Press, 1988). This book summarizes and extends facts and viewpoints developed in numerous articles and reviews by McWhiney and Forrest McDonald.

18. J. Hector St. John de Crèvecoeur, *Letters from an American Farmer,* Everyman's Library (1912), 43.

19. Fischer, *Albion's Seed,* 889.

20. Ibid., 873.

21. "Albion's Seed: Four British Folkways in America—A Symposium," *William and Mary Quarterly* 48 (April 1991): 223–308. Contributors are Jack P. Greene, Virginia DeJohn Anderson, James Horn, Barry Levy, Ned C. Landmore, and David Hackett Fischer.

Chapter 3: Southern Ethnics

1. U. S. Department of Commerce, Bureau of the Census, *Statistical Abstract of the United States: 1992* (Washington, D.C.: U. S. Department of Commerce, 1992), 10; U. S. Department of Justice, Immigration and Naturalization Service, *Immigration Statistics: Fiscal Year 1991* (leaflet, Washington, D.C.: U. S. Department of Justice, 1992), 1.

2. David M. Reimers, *Still the Golden Door: The Third World Comes to America* (New York: Columbia University Press, 1985), 7; Leonard Dinnerstein and David M. Reimers, *Ethnic Americans: A History of Immigration,* 3d ed. (New York: Harper and Row, 1988), 85–88.

3. Reimers, *Still the Golden Door,* 11–38; Dinnerstein and Reimers, *Ethnic Americans,* 88–90.

4. A useful summary of this legislation (except for 1990) may be found in Scott McConnell, "The New Battle Over Immigration," *Fortune* 117 (May 9 1988): 89–102. Greater detail appears in Reimers, *Still the Golden Door,* 20–22, 26–27, 63–90.

5. H. Eugene Douglas, "Landing in the Land of the Free," *American Demographics* 4 (August 1984): 29.

6. Quoted in Aaron Siegel, "The Half-Open Door," *Wilson Quarterly* 7 (New Year's 1983): 119.

7. Scott McConnell, "The New Battle over Immigration," 98.

8. *Facts on File* 46 (1986): 814B2, 853B3.

9. Ibid., 50 (1990): 814F3–815F1. Quotation from *Time* 138 (October 14, 1992): 27. A similar paraphrase of Emma Lazarus appeared in "Give Us Your Brainpower," *U. S. News and World Report* 109 (October 29, 1990): 108.

10. Hajimu Sasaki to Eric J. Gangloff, July 31, 1987. Letter from a professor of English at Tohoku University, Sendai,

Japan, to the associate executive director of the Japan-United States Friendship Commission, Tokyo, restating opinions expressed by Yoshimitsu Ide, professor of history at Tokyo Women's University. Copy in possession of the author.

11. Ezra F. Vogel, *Comeback. Case by Case: Building the Resurgence of American Business* (New York: Simon and Schuster, 1985), 240–62.

12. Alma Guerrero, "A Better Future: Mexican Women in North Carolina," seminar paper, Department of History, University of North Carolina at Chapel Hill, 1989. Copy in possession of the author.

13. Kirkpatrick Sale, *Power Shift: The Rise of the Southern Rim and Its Challenge to the Eastern Establishment* (New York: Random House, 1975); James R. Adams, "The Sunbelt," *Dixie Dateline: A Journalistic Portrait of the Contemporary South,* ed. John B. Boles (Houston, Tex.: Rice University Studies, 1983), 142.

14. "South Carolina Hills Are Alive With Euro-Commerce," *Washington Post,* December 26, 1992, A1:2, A15:1–6; "The Boom Belt," *Business Week,* September 27, 1993, 98–104. Quotation from *Washington Post.*

15. Computed from *Census of 1940: Population* (Washington, D.C.: Bureau of the Census, 1943), II, 88; *Census of 1960, Population* (Washington, D.C.: Bureau of the Census, 1964), I, 1–16, 1–201, 1–625; *Statistical Abstract of the United States: 1992,* 42; *1990 Census of Population and Housing,* Summary Tape File #3C on CD-ROM Technical Documentation (Washington, D.C.: Bureau of the Census, 1993); and Donald J. Bogue, *The Population of the United States: Historical Trends and Future Projections* (New York: The Free Press, 1985), 371. See also John D. Kasarda, Michael D. Irwin, and Holly L. Hughes, "The South is Still Rising," *American Demographics* 8 (June 1986): 32–39, 70.

16. Otis L. Graham, Jr., "From Snowbelt to Sunbelt: The Impact of Migration," *Dialogue*, no. 39 (January 1983): 10; *Statistical Abstract of the United States: 1992*, 21–22.

17. Isaac Robinson, "Blacks Move Back to the South," *American Demographics* 8 (June 1986): 40–43.

18. *Chapel Hill [NC] Newspaper,* December 4, 1988, C–5.

19. Randall M. Miller and George E. Pozzetta, eds., *Shades of the Sunbelt: Essays on Ethnicity, Race, and the Urban South* (New York: Greenwood Press, 1988). See also Raymond A. Mohl, ed., *Searching for the Sunbelt: Historical Perspectives on a Region* (Knoxville: University of Tennessee Press, 1990); Richard M. Bernard and Bradley R. Rice, *Sunbelt Cities: Politics and Growth Since World War II* (Austin: University of Texas Press, 1983); and Barbara Carpenter, ed., *Ethnic Heritage in Mississippi* (Jackson: University Press of Mississippi, 1992). Newer titles will be reported in the *Journal of American Ethnic History* and *Immigration Newsletter.*

20. A likely selection of useful recent books on Miami would include Joan Didion, *Miami* (New York: Simon and Schuster, 1987); T. D. Allman, *Miami, City of the Future* (New York: Atlantic Monthly Press, 1987); David Rieff, *Going to Miami: Exiles, Tourists, and Refugees in the New America* (Boston: Little Brown, 1987); and Guillermo J. Grenier and Alex Stepick III, eds., *Miami Now!: Immigration, Ethnicity, and Social Change* (Gainesville: University of Florida Press, 1992).

21. Daniels, *A Southerner Discovers the South*, 313.

22. Raymond A. Mohl, "Ethnic Politics in Miami, 1960–1986," in Miller and Pozzetta, *Shades of the Sunbelt,* pp. 143–60; David Goldfield and Howard N. Rabinowitz, "The Vanishing Sunbelt," in Mohl, *Searching for the Sunbelt,* 226.

23. Raymond Arsenault and Gary R. Mormino, "From Dixie

to Dreamland: Demographic and Cultural Change in Florida, 1880–1980," in Miller and Pozzetta, *Shades of the Sunbelt,* 161–91. *Statistical Abstract of the United States: 1992,* 23.

24. Ibid., 134–36; Ronald H. Bayor, "Models of Ethnic and Racial Politics in the Urban Sunbelt South," in Mohl, *Searching for the Sunbelt,* 115. See also David A. Johnson, John A. Booth, and Richard J. Harris, *The Politics of San Antonio: Community, Progress, and Power* (Lincoln: University of Nebraska Press, 1983).

25. Earl Shorris, *Latinos: A Biography of the People* (New York: Norton, 1992), 37.

26. *Houston Chronicle,* September 11, 1988.

27. Tindall, "Beyond the Mainstream," 8. There is a literature on local ethnic groups too extensive to summarize here; much information is given in the entries under George E. Pozzetta (consultant), "Ethnicity," in *Encyclopedia of Southern Culture,* ed. Charles Reagan Wilson and William Ferris (Chapel Hill: University of North Carolina Press, 1989), 401–45. See also Miller and Pozzetta, *Shades of the Sunbelt.* Of particular interest is J. Anthony Paredes, ed., *Indians of the Southeastern United States in the Late Twentieth Century* (Tuscaloosa: University of Alabama Press, 1992).

28. John Smith, *The Proceedings of the English Colony in Virginia . . .* (Oxford, England, 1612), reprinted in *The Complete Works of Captain John Smith (1580–1631),* ed. Philip L. Barber (Chapel Hill: University of North Carolina Press, 1986), 1: 246.

29. Quoted in Dinnerstein and Reimers, *Ethnic Americans,* 6.

30. Marilyn T. Grunkemeyer, "A Vietnamese-American Community: An Instance of Moral Education," Ph.D. dissertation, University of North Carolina at Chapel Hill, 1991.

31. Ronald H. Bayor, "Race, Ethnicity, and Political Change

in the Urban South," in Miller and Pozzetta, *Shades of the Sunbelt*, 131.

32. Max J. Castro, "The Politics of Language in Miami," in *Miami Now!*, 109–32; see also Ronald H. Bayor, "Models of Ethnic and Racial Politics in the Urban Sunbelt South," in Miller and Pozzetta, *Searching for the Sunbelt*, 110–11.

33. Marcus Lee Hansen, *The Problem of the Third Generation Immigrant* (Rock Island, Ill.: Augustana Historical Society, 1938), 9–10.

34. Dan Foot, "American Indians in the 1890s," *American Demographics* 13 (December 1991): 26–33.

35. Raymond A. Mohl, "Miami: New Immigrant City," in *Searching for the Sunbelt*, 163–68; Thomas Exter, "The Spanish Future," *American Demographics* 11 (October 1989): 63. Exter cites *The Future of the Spanish Language in the United States* from the Hispanic Policy Development Project.

36. James L. Peacock III, "Multiple Cultures in the South," typescript draft proposal for a symposium on "The Multicultural South," which took place at the University of North Carolina at Chapel Hill, April 8, 1989. Typescript, 1989, in possession of the author.

Index

Index

Index

Index